Our Mother's Tears:

Ten Weeping Madonnas in Historic Hungary

By Erika Papp Faber

To Darlene –
who gave me my
first interview –
with love, Erika

ACADEMY OF THE IMMACULATE
NEW BEDFORD, MA
2006

June 28, 2009,

Our Mother's Tears: Ten Weeping Madonnas in Historic Hungary is a book prepared for publication by the Franciscans of the Immaculate [marymediatrix.com]. POB 3003, New Bedford, MA, 02741-3003.

Cum permissu superiorum

ISBN: 1-60114-031-2

Contents

Introduction

From its inception as a Christian nation over a thousand years ago, Hungary has had a fervent devotion to Mary, the Mother of God. The first king, St. Stephen, offered his crown, and thereby his country, to Her protection in 1038. She is *Patrona Hungariae,* Patroness of Hungary, and *Magna Domina Hungarorum*, the Great Lady of the Hungarians. A publication which appeared towards the end of the second millennium* lists 200 Marian shrines in a country that today is a mere 36,000 square miles, but historically was a total 125,641 square miles when these Marian images wept within its borders.

There are records of Marian paintings weeping tears in Hungary as early as 1663. (Although ten are revered as having shed tears, I have found records of only nine; one of the ten is based merely on a legend, and has no documentation.) Often, the original was removed from the location where it first was seen to weep, to the consternation of the local populace. Then copies were made to replace the original. In one case, that of Máriapócs, when the original weeping icon was transferred to Vienna, Austria, the copy sent to replace it wept also, not just once, but twice: in 1715 and again in 1905. (This, by the way, was the last recorded weeping.) For this reason, I have counted it twice, (the original and the copy) for a total of ten Weeping Madonnas.

Four of the Weeping Madonnas were icons in Byzantine rite Catholic churches, and each one of these was a painting of a Madonna and Child. The rest were in Roman rite Catholic churches.

Why did these Marian images weep? While no one can know the mind of God or of Mary, some have tried to make a connection with the political events of the time. I too will hazard some conjectures along this line.

Some of the Weeping Madonnas had an adventurous history, others less so, but each one's story is unique. And it may be considered an honor bestowed by the Mother of God on the Hungarian people to have so many of Her images shed tears within its borders. This booklet has been compiled to acknowledge Mary's concern for Her people and to thank Her for this singular privilege.

Könnyező Édesanyánk, könyörögj érettünk! Our Weeping Mother, pray for us! Amen.

*"Mária kegyhelyek Mária országában" ("Marian Shrines in Mary's Country") by J. Krizosztom Ipolyvölgyi Németh, Budapest, 1998.

Acknowledgements

Many people, in the United States, Canada and in Europe, have helped me gather not only the information, but more importantly, the photographs of the Weeping Madonnas. Without their help, this work could not have been completed.

I wish to thank the following for their kind assistance: Baroness Éva Bálintitt of Staten Island, NY who, through family contacts, accessed the pictures from Kolozsvár; Rev. Pál Cséfalvay of Esztergom's Vizivárosi templom, for the picture of the Nagyszombat copy there; the late Rev. István Cser-Palkovits, SJ, of Vienna, Austria, for much background information; the Very Rev. József Erdey, OSBM, Superior of the Basilian Fathers at the Shrine of Máriapócs, Matawan, NJ, who was so patient with my persistent pestering; Rev. Balázs Figeczki, Pastor, Byzantine Catholic Church of Sajópálfala, Hungary, for the "rest of the story" about that Weeping Madonna; Sr.Flora, S.M., who provided valuable information about the Shrine of Máriapoch in Burton, OH; Mr. Alfred Freunschlag Jr. for his photograph of the Weeping Madonna located in Wiener Neustadt, Austria, and of the cathedral there; Mr. and Mrs. Sándor Károlyi, of Zebegény, Hungary, for their input, and for personally traveling to the shrine of Bácsfa-Szentantal in Slovakia, and obtaining pictures for me; Ms. Helen Kenderesi, of South Norwalk, CT for the text of some of the hymns used; Mark Koleszar of Park Studios, G-ville, OH, for the photos of the Burton OH shrine; Mr. Norbert Koppensteiner, Director of the

Wiener Neustadt City Museum, for information and for steering me in the right direction; Rev. József Márk, of Csíksomlyó, Romania, who set me straight about that Madonna; Ms. Márta Máthé, of Tirgu-Mures, Romania, who received permission to open the window and take a photograph of the Weeping Madonna of Kolozsvár, and who got Mr. Zágon Szentes (Szentes Zágon) to take the photograph used here; Rev. Lajos Meskó, Sch.P., of Devon, PA, whose listing "Magyar szentek, boldogok és szentéletű magyarok jegyzéke" gave me the original idea to compile this study; the Most Rev. Attila Miklósházy, SJ, Bishop of Hungarians Abroad, of Scarborough, ONT, Canada, for the names of contacts and for providing encouragement; Dr. Marcell Mosolygó, Pastor of the Byzantine Catholic Parish of Máriapócs, Hungary, who corrected my information about that shrine; Rev. István Mustos, Sch. P., Pastor, Passaic, NJ, for his referrals; Mr. Zoltán Nagy of the web page www.búcsújárás.hu, for permission to use their photo of the Nagyszombat picture; Ms. Loretta Nemeth of the Byzantine Catholic Eparchy of Parma, OH, who contacted the photographer and provided much background information for the Burton, OH shrine; Ms. Zuzana Olejnikova of the Secretariat of the Slovak Bishops' Conference, for the very elusive picture of sv. Mikulasa church in Trnava; Miss Teresa Petrak, of Astoria, NY, who commissioned her relatives in Slovakia to obtain the pictures from Klokocsó; Rev. Mátyás Schindler, of Baja, Hungary, for photos and information about Baja-Máriakönnye; Miss Bernadette Végh, of Szécsény, Hungary, for a modern reference work about Hungarian Marian shrines; Mr. Pál Vincze, of Budapest, Hungary, for books and other background material, and information about Jánoshida; and Ms.

Sudárka Vossler, for the pictures of St. Anthony of Padua Church, Winnipeg, Canada.

Thanks are due also to: the Parish Office of Vizivárosi templom, Esztergom, Hungary; the Diocesan Office of Győr; and to St. Stephen of Hungary Church, Toledo, OH.

May Our Mother of Tears bless all of them for their kind assistance in making Her better known!

List of Weeping Madonnas in Historic Hungary

Bácsfa-Szent Antal

Baja-Máriakönnye

Győr

Királyfalva

Klokocsó

Kolozsvár

Máriapócs I

Máriapócs II

Nagyszombat

Pálfalva

N.B.   According to popular belief, the miraculous statue of Our Lady at the shrine of **Csíksomlyó,** Transylvania also shed tears. However, the Franciscan Superior, Fr. József Márk, has assured me that such is *not* the case: **"There is no mention, in writing nor in tradition, of the statue's weeping at Csíksomlyó.** Other phenomena have been recorded, for example, the statue has glowed, shone, its face was sad, which was always followed by some catastrophe or war. Very many prayers are being answered through the intercession of the Virgin Mother, even to our day. **But weeping is not mentioned anywhere.**"

Chronological Table of Weepings

Byz=Byzantine Catholic; RC=Roman Catholic; M&C=Mother&Child

1663 Nagyszombat	RC	Mary blessing	Tears	Battle of Párkány
1670 Klokocsó	Byz	M&C	Tears	Political persecution
1683 Királyfalva	RC	Pieta	Mary cried, Jesus sweated	Turks driven from Vienna
1696 Máriapócs I	Byz	M&C	Tears	Sobieski's victory over Turks
1697 Győr	RC	Mary w. sleeping Infant	Tears & bloody sweat	Oppression, poverty in Hungary; persecution in Ireland
1699 Kolozsvár	Byz	M&C	Tears	Austria gains control over Hungary & Transylvania
1708 Nagyszombat	RC	Mary blessing	Tears & bloody sweat	Plague, insurrection
1715 (copy) Máriapócs II	Byz	M&C	Tears	Beginning of Austria's policy of "Germanizing" Hungary
1715 Bácsfa-Szt. Antal	RC	M&C	Bloody tears	
1717 Pálfalva	Byz	M&C	Bloody tears & sweat	Turks driven out of southern Hungary
1905 (copy) Máriapócs II	Byz	M&C	Tears	Divorce legalized
???? Baja-Máriakönnye	RC & Byz	M&C	*Legend* of tears turning into a spring (or springs)	

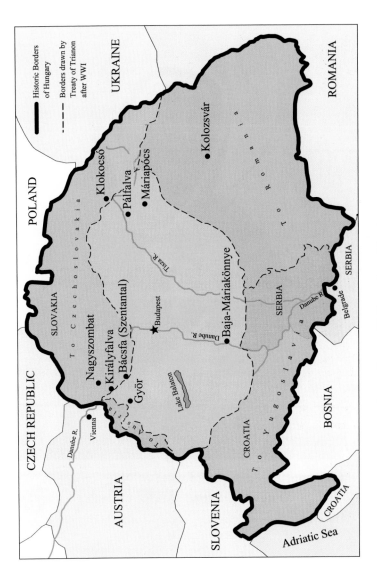

Location of Weeping Madonnas

**Original Weeping Madonna of Nagyszombat/
Trnava in Szent Miklós church**

(Courtesy of Mr. Zoltán Nagy/Nagy Zoltán of the web page
www.búcsújárás.hu)

Nagyszombat

Location: Nagyszombat, Pozsony County

Present-day national jurisdiction: Slovakia; present-day name: Trnava

Name of Church: Szent Miklós

Rite: Roman Catholic

Type of image: Painting of Mary with her hand raised in blessing

Dates of weeping: 1663 & 1708

Copy: made in 1820, located in Esztergom

History: Ferenc Forgách, who later became cardinal, had the picture copied, in the 16th century, from a miraculous painting revered in the Church of St. Alexis in Rome. After having it blessed and touched it to the original, he brought it home to Hungary, and donated it to the Church of Szent Miklós in Nagyszombat. That was where the Chapter of Esztergom Cathedral was located at the time.

In 1663, this picture shed tears, prior to the bloody battle of Párkány. At that time, the Blessed Mother saved the city from destruction by the Turks, by sending a dense fog over the region. The inhabitants of Nagyszombat therefore honor Her as their heavenly Protectress.

By the turn of the century, Hungary was suffering from religious warfare and the devastations of the plague. In the midst of these troubles, the city of Nagyszombat heard rumors of another miraculous occurrence.

On July 5th, August 10th and August 11th, 1708, the Weeping Madonna shed tears again, and was seen to perspire. At 5 AM on August 11th, 1708, the pastor of the church touched the tears which he saw Our Lady shed, to convince himself of the reality of the prodigy.

Great numbers of people repented when they witnessed the weeping of Mary's picture, convinced that their sins were the reason for their many hardships, which even Our Lady deemed worthy of tears.

Thirty eyewitnesses gave sworn testimony to the truth of the miraculous weeping. Many then recalled the earlier episode of weeping, in 1663, which had not been widely publicized before.

After thorough investigation, the Church put its seal of approval on the miracle by granting an indulgence to those who visit the miraculous picture, under the usual conditions. The decree is dated November 21, 1710, the day the plague ended, following an intercessory procession with the miraculously weeping picture.

In 1820, the Archbishop's seat was transferred to Esztergom. A copy was made of the Weeping Madonna of Nagyszombat, and the Canons brought it with them. The basilica of Esztergom had not been built yet, so they placed the copy in the church of St. Ignatius of Loyola, popularly known as "Vizivárosi templom", where it may be seen to this day.

Hymn to the Weeping Madonna of Nagyszombat

To the Virgin Mary we've come in greeting,
To our dearest heavenly Mother weeping!
Our souls are wide open with devotion,
Our lips pay homage with glad emotion.

To you, our good Mother, this song brings
  our thanks,
Because the world's troubles cause you such
  great pangs,
For so much grief over human hearts hangs,
Relief only your holy heart can grant.

Upon us break the miseries of our age,
Jealousy and hatred mar our very souls,
Our hearts are anxious about tomorrow.
Your precious tears are our only solace.

Upon the cross your holy Son died for us,
Breaking thereby hell's chains nefarious,
Let's also smash our sinful impetus,
For our faith will soar aloft only thus.

O weeping Mother dear, we beg you, teach us
To cry only if our sins are numerous,
We need not tremble in the stormy night,
If we trust your and your Son's heart aright.

We'll win, for God is with us with His great
    might,
And the blood and the tears are so strong
    indeed,
You and Jesus are our holy portion,
Together through this faith we'll win the
    fight.

O holy Virgin, your dear tears teach us thus:
Let's finally kiss our crosses onerous.
In fond farewell we bow before you now,
Accept the loyalty your children vow.

Church of Szt. Miklós (sv. Mikulasa) where the
Weeping Madonna of Nagyszombat (Trnava) is
located, in present-day Slovakia.

(Courtesy Ms. Zuzana Olejnikova, Secretariat, Slovak Bishops'
Conference)

**Copy of Weeping Madonna of Nagyszombat,
located in Esztergom**

(Courtesy of Rev. Pál Cséfalvay/Cséfalvay Pál)

"Vizivárosi templom" (Church of St. Ignatius of
Loyola) in Esztergom, where copy of the Weeping
Madonna of Nagyszombat is located

(Courtesy of Parish Office, Vizivárosi templom)

Second copy of Weeping Madonna of Klokocsó
(Courtesy Miss Teresa Petrak)

Klokocsó

Location: Klokocsó (also known as Hajagos), in Nagymihály district, Zemplén County

Present-day national jurisdiction: Slovakia; present-day name: Klokochovo, in Michalovci district

Name of church: Dormition of the Holy Mother of God

Rite: Byzantine Catholic

Type of image: Icon – Painting of Mother and Child with crowns

Date of weeping: 1670

Original: Removed to the town hall of Eperjes;

then to the Chapel of Munkács Castle, by Countess Zsófia Báthory;

then to Nicomedia (present-day Izmit, Turkey), by the Countess Helen Zrinyi, in 1688;

returned to Munkács Castle, in 1703;

taken to private chapel of imperial palace in Vienna;

now missing.

Copy: painted by F. Kramer – placed in Eperjes city hall in 1769;

donated to Bishop John Vályi of Eperjes in 1904, installed in Bishop's chapel in 1907.

Second copy: commissioned by Bishop Vályi; painted by local artist István Roskovics donated to Klokocsó church in 1913

> **Text** under the painting reads: "True picture of the Blessed Mother, located in the village church of Klokocsó, belonging to the Castle of Vinna in Upper Hungary, which in 1670 was seen by many first to weep, then, following the stabbing with a knife by some heretics, to shed tears that flowed down her cheeks."

History: In 1670, Hungarian Protestant troops, which were trying to free Hungary of Catholic Hapsburg rule, were approaching Klokocsó. The people of the town fled to the church, imploring the assistance of Mary, "Help of Christians." As they were praying, they noticed that the icon was shedding tears. They prayed all the more fervently. The "kurucok", as the troops called themselves, burst into the church, and started to destroy all religious objects. One of the soldiers pierced the icon with his bayonet, at which the tears flowed even more profusely. Enraged, the soldier tore the icon out of the iconostasis and threw it on the floor to trample it. But the parishioners came to the rescue, pushing the soldier aside, and someone picked up the icon and ran into the woods with it. The soldiers burned down the wooden church, but the weeping icon was saved.

Once the troops had left, the parishioners brought the weeping icon to the town hall of Eperjes for safekeeping, until they could rebuild their church.

The town of Eperjes was located on the lands owned by the Rákóczi family. The hereditary Prince was still a minor at the time, and the family estate was administered by his mother, Countess Sophia Báthory. Once she had heard about the miraculous weeping of the icon, she ordered it brought to her castle in Munkács (Mukachevo), and had it placed over the altar in the chapel. She became very devoted to the icon, and adorned it with precious stones and drapery.

Upon the death of the Countess Báthory, the Countess Helen Zrinyi became the sole administrator of the estate. She remarried, becoming the wife of Imre Thököly, the leader of the Hungarian insurrection. He was defeated, and had to take refuge in Turkey. His wife was allowed to join him there, which is how the miraculously weeping icon of Klokocsó was taken to Nicomedia (Izmit), Turkey.

After the death of the Countess Zrinyi, the miraculous icon was returned to Munkács castle by her son Francis Rákóczy II. When he also joined the insurrection against the Hapsburgs and was defeated, he too had to seek refuge in Turkey. All the treasures of the Rákóczi family were confiscated and taken to the imperial court in Vienna.

Repeated requests for the return of the miraculously weeping icon went unheeded. Eventually, the Empress Maria Theresa had a copy made, and sent it to Eperjes. The icon copy stayed there until 1904, when it was donated to Bishop Vályi of Eperjes. The bishop would not part with the icon copy, but instead had a second copy (a copy of the copy!) made for the church of

Klokocsó, which then became the center of pilgrimages in the Munkács eparchy.

After World War I, Upper Hungary, including Klokocsó, became part of Czechoslovakia.

During World War II, pilgrimages to Klokocsó declined, particularly because of bomb damage to the church and rectory. After World War II, Klokocsó was placed under the jurisdiction of the bishop of Eperjes (Prjashev). The church and rectory were rebuilt, and pilgrimages resumed in 1946. But not for long. In 1949, the Communist authorities forbade all pilgrimages. They were resumed only after the so-called "Velvet Revolution" of 1989, when Communism was defeated.

From: "Hymn about the Weeping Icon of Klokocsó"

– a handwritten manuscript of a poem describing the burning of Klokocsó church by the "kurucok" , found in the neighboring village of Kövecske (Kamiemka):

> Weeping was the icon
> Of the Most Pure in Klokochovo,
> Then was taken and placed
> In the castle of Mukachevo!
> (1683)

Poem/Prayer Accompanying Sketch of Church

Three hundred years ago, this Maria cried over the people of Zemplén. Her tears flowed. Maria, Maria, intercede for us with your Son, be gracious to us, save Zemplén!

Pred tristo rokmi, hľa,
Mária plakala, nad ľudom
Zemplína slzy prelievala.
Mária, Mária, pros za nás u Syna,
buď nám milostivá, ochrana Zemplína!

Obraz Bohorodičky v chráme obce Klokočov,
ktorý v roku 1670 slzil,
keď ho zneuctili a nožom prebodli heretici.

Sketch of Klokocsó Church, with poem/prayer.
This is where the second copy of the Weeping
Madonna is located (present-day Slovakia).

(Courtesy of Miss Teresa Petrak)

Weeping Madonna of Királyfalva, now located in
the Cathedral of Wiener Neustadt, Austria

(Photograph by Alfred Freunschlag Jr.)

Királyfalva (Királyfa)

Location: (originally known as Királyfalva), Pozsony County, Szencz District

Present-day national jurisdiction: Slovakia; present-day name: Kralová pri Senice

Name of church: Chapel of Pálffy Castle

Rite: Roman Catholic

Type of image: Pietà (Sorrowful Mother holding Her dead Son)

Date of weeping: 1683

Original: Removed to Wiener Neustadt, Austria

Copy: Made for the people of Királyfalva

History: The picture, in the style of 16th century Dutch painting, is of a Pietà (the Sorrowful Mother with Her dead Son in Her lap). It was located in the chapel of the Pálffy castle at Királyfalva, a small village in Pozsony County. At the time of the Turkish occupation of Vienna in 1683, the area of Pozsony and Királyfalva itself was threatened by enemy troops. It was then that the picture was seen by many people, including those of the high nobility, to be shedding copious tears, while the figure of Jesus in Her lap was seen to perspire.

The Hapsburg emperor ordered the picture to be brought to Austria. It was placed on the main altar of the (then) Jesuit church in Wiener Neustadt. From there, it was moved to the cathedral of Wiener Neustadt in 1775, and received a place of honor over the main altar. In 1960, it was moved to a baroque chapel that opens from the north transept to the left of the main altar.

Before being taken away, a copy was painted on wooden boards for the people of Királyfalva.

The owners of Pálffy castle pledged themselves in perpetuity to engage a Capuchin friar for the service of the chapel. The local, mostly Slovak, population had free access to the chapel and to the copy of the miraculous picture, and could even assemble for Sunday afternoon litanies and recitation of the rosary there. It was always jammed full, as pilgrims came from the surrounding countryside, and even from as far away as Csallóköz.

It is not known what became of this copy in the turbulence of the 20th century.

**Cathedral of Wiener Neustadt, Austria, where the
Weeping Madonna of Királyfalva is now located**
(Photograph by Alfred Freunschlag Jr.)

Original Weeping Madonna of Máriapócs, now located in Vienna, Austria

(Verlag Richard Pietsch & Co. KG, Wien)

Máriapócs

Location: Pócs (now Máriapócs), formerly Szabolcs, now Szabolcs-Szatmár County

Present-day national jurisdiction: Hungary

Name of church: St. Michael the Archangel

Rite: Byzantine Catholic

Type of image: Icon – Mother and Child

Dates of weeping:
> 1696 by original icon in Máriapócs, Hungary (#I)
> 1715 by copy in Máriapócs (#II)
> 1905 by copy in Máriapócs (#II)

Original: Removed to St. Stephen's Cathedral in Vienna, Austria

Copy: Venerated in Máriapócs, Hungary

History: A villager named László Csigri had an icon of the Mother of God painted for the iconostasis of the Byzantine Catholic church at Pócs, in thanksgiving for having escaped from Turkish captivity. As Csigri was unable to pay the six Hungarian gold pieces for the finished icon, a wealthy parishioner named Lőrincz Hurta paid for it and donated it to the church.

On November 4, 1696, the icon began to weep during the Sacred Liturgy. The priest wiped away the tears with a silk cloth which he gave to the bishop of Eger. (The bishop then donated it to the Jesuits of that city. After the Jesuits were sent away in 1707, the cloth was carried in procession in Kassa, Gyöngyös as well as in Eger. In 1820, the Holy See decided to exhibit the cloth with the copy of the weeping Madonna in the Archbishop's church in Eger.)

The weeping continued for two weeks, during which time many prayers were answered and many cures recorded. One of the most spectacular occurred when the Roman Catholic priest of a neighboring village lifted a dying child to the weeping icon, and the child recovered after touching the tears streaming from Mary's eyes. The grateful mother brought a necklace of precious stones, the first of many such thank offerings which in time covered the entire picture.

On December 8th, 1696, on a day so cold the wine froze in the priest's chalice, the icon began to weep again. The tears continued to flow for 11 days, during which time Church and government officials examined the picture and interrogated witnesses to determine the authenticity of the miracle. Witnesses included not only Catholics, but also Protestants and even a Muslim Turkish soldier who was so touched by Mary's tears that he converted to the Catholic faith and settled in the village which, since the icon's weeping, has been called Máriapócs.

As happened in the case of Királyfalva, when the Austrian emperor heard of the miraculously weeping picture, he had it arbitrarily removed from the church of Máriapócs and brought to Vienna, Austria, despite the objections of the local inhabitants. The icon's journey stretched to several months, as people all along its route paid homage to it. Arriving in Vienna, the painting was received with great pomp and devotion, and placed over the main altar of St. Stephen's Roman Catholic Cathedral.

In the course of the next 40 years, close to 300 cures and miracles were recorded in connection with the weeping icon the Austrians came to call "Maria Pötsch". Attributed to it also was the defeat of the overwhelming Turkish forces at Zenta in 1697, for which the entire population sent up prayers to the Mother of the miraculous image. So many votive thank offerings were made that later on, when these were melted down, they were sufficient to make a silver altar and 38 artistic picture frames.

The Vienna City Council established a foundation of 600 florins, for the sole purpose of celebrating a daily festive Mass in honor of the Weeping Madonna.

During World War II, St. Stephen's Cathedral in Vienna was so severely damaged by bombs that the roof caved in. Nevertheless, the miraculously weeping icon of Máriapócs was untouched. It was restored after World War II, and the numerous votive offerings which had been attached to it were removed. At the same time, the following inscription came to light: "I, a servant of God, had this picture set up for the forgiveness of my sins." These words had probably been added at the request of László Csigri, who had originally ordered the painting.

Today, the icon is venerated at its own altar located near the front right entrance of St. Stephen's Cathedral in Vienna. The multitude of candles burning before it even now attests to the enduring devotion of the people to Our Lady of Máriapócs.

A copy promised by the emperor to the villagers of Máriapócs duly replaced the original weeping icon. Then, on August 1st, 1715, this copy also began to shed tears in the church of Máriapócs, Hungary. Many hundreds witnessed the weeping which was repeated on August 2nd and 5th for several hours. By the 5th, the weeping was so voluminous, that the tears covered the Virgin Mother's face, chest and hands as well. Again, the miracle was verified by a Church tribunal and declared authentic.

A wealthy nobleman donated two crowns to adorn the Infant and Mary, and a protective covering was placed over the painting, leaving only the faces open to view. Many votive offerings of thanksgiving were attached to this cover, proof of the innumerable miracles of all kinds which were obtained through devotion to this _second_ weeping icon of Máriapócs (# II).

The wooden church of Máriapócs soon proved to be too small to accommodate all the pilgrims wishing to see the second miraculously weeping icon. In time, a large stone church was erected on the site in 1756, but the towers were completed only a century later, in 1856.

On December 3rd, 1905, this second picture in Máriapócs shed tears once more. It continued weeping until December 19th, and wept again the last two days of December 1905. The cloth catching the tears was placed in a small frame and can still be seen on the wall of the church.

Members of the committee investigating this new manifestation of the Virgin's sorrow included doctors and scientists, Catholic theologians as well as Protestants and Jews. Once again, the miraculous tears were declared authentic.

Pope Pius XII raised the church of Máriapócs to the status of a basilica in 1946. József Cardinal Mindszenty, Archbishop of Esztergom and Primate of Hungary, was the principal celebrant of the Liturgy marking the occasion. The celebration also commemorated the 250th anniversary of the original icon's weeping, and the 300th anniversary of the Union of Ungvár (Uzhgorod), which united the region's Orthodox Christians with the Church of Rome.

Soon thereafter, the Communist regime came to power in Hungary. Religious processions were forbidden and the roads leading to Máriapócs were blocked. For many years, it was dangerous to go there ; those who did go were subject to political harassment. The toppling of the Communist government, in 1989, opened the way to pilgrimages once again. Votive offerings are found at Our Lady's altar afresh, and 30-40 tablets of thanksgiving, testifying to prayers answered, are added by the faithful every year.

Pope John Paul II visited the shrine of Máriapócs in 1991, and celebrated a Byzantine rite Liturgy in Hungarian, in front of the miraculous icon.

The diocesan bishop declared 2005 to be a jubilee year, commemorating the 100th anniversary of the icon's last weeping. In addition, the icon would travel around the country, leaving Máriapócs for the first time.

Although one of the smallest towns in Hungary, with a mere 2,800 inhabitants, Máriapócs is the largest place of pilgrimage of the entire Byzantine Catholic Church, drawing over half a million pilgrims annually.

Our Lady of Máriapócs is also venerated in Austria, Germany and Switzerland.

In the U.S., the Basilian Fathers maintain shrines in her honor in Matawan, NJ and Burton, Ohio. The Greek Catholic Church of St. John the Baptist in Perth Amboy, NJ is a copy of the basilica of Máriapócs; so is the Byzantine Catholic Church of SS. Peter and Paul in Punxsutawney, PA, but there the steeples have been replaced by domes. Numerous other Byzantine Catholic churches, and at least two Russian Orthodox churches in the U.S. have Máriapócs shrines or icons.

Máriapócs Pilgrims' Hymn

Welcome! God brought you, pious and
    devout faithful, to this holy place,
Where the sweet, good Virgin Mother awaits
    you with joy.

Refrain:
Virgin Mary, Pearl of Heaven, your faithful
    ones now bless.
With your precious hands press us to your
    heart.

Here in the beautiful church of Pócs she
    distributes blessings plentifully,
Hears the prayers of those whose heart is
    true and pure.
Refrain

Accept kindly, our heavenly Mother, this
  our pilgrimage,
Which we now offer to you in this holy
  place.
Refrain

Prayer to Our Lady of Máriapócs

O my weeping Mother, refuge of sinners, I beg
you, for the sake of your tears, to obtain for me
from Jesus the forgiveness of my sins, and the
blessings of your holy Son upon me and mine.
Ease our sufferings, heal our ills, console us in
our sorrows, help us to lead virtuous lives, and
lead us finally into the happiness of heaven.

O weeping Virgin, dear Mother of God,
remember us before Jesus, now and at the hour
of our death. Amen.

From a Litany Used in Burton, Ohio

...Rejoice, O Weeping Mother of God, who had
shed tears for us sinners at Mariapoch (sic).
Help and save all who have recourse to you...

O most Blessed Virgin, Mother of mercy, Mary
adorned with miracles, who shed tears on the
holy ground of Mariapoch; we, who honor
you, humbly beseech you for your motherly
shelter; save our country from all enemies, lift
up our Church and in peace and one faith join
all churches, that at last there may be one flock
and one shepherd.

Do not deny your intercession before your Holy Son, beseech for us peaceful times, the blessing of our labor, health for our bodies, peace for our souls. Intercede for us, that our last hour may find us in the Catholic faith and in perfect sorrow, and that we may gain eternal salvation. Amen.

As we go to press, the following developments must be added:

The icon of the Weeping Madonna of Máriapócs was restored by experts for the 2005 centenary of its last weeping. The covering veil was removed. A "crown", blessed by Pope Benedict XVI, was placed on it. Actually, this is merely a gold overlay covering the halo that was painted on the icon. In December 2005,Péter Cardinal Erdő declared the church of Máriapócs a national shrine.

St. Stephen's Cathedral (Stephansdom), Vienna, Austria, where the original Weeping Madonna of Máriapócs is located

(Verlag P. Ledermann, Wien)

Copy of original Weeping Madonna of Máriapócs
with its protective covering and votive offerings, in
Máriapócs, Hungary

(Photo by Miklós Erdős/Erdős Miklós, published in "A
Könnyező Máriapócsi Szűzanya csodatevő kegyképe")

Pilgrimage church of Máriapócs, Hungary, where
the copy of the original Weeping Madonna is
venerated. This copy has also shed tears, twice.

(Photo by Miklós Erdős/Erdős Miklós)

Mosaic copy of the Weeping Madonna of Máriapócs at the Monastery of the Basilian Fathers in Matawan, NJ. Unfortunately, it was damaged by the weather, and is no longer displayed there.

(Photo by Erika Papp Faber)

Monastery of the Basilian Fathers of Máriapócs at Matawan, NJ

(Photo by Edmond Geisler, pub. by EGee Studio of Photography, Rahway, NJ)

Shrine of Our Lady of Mariapoch (sic), Burton, OH. Each is a mosaic rendition of the Weeping Madonna of Máriapócs. On the left is a copy of the original Weeping Madonna (now in Vienna); on the right, a copy of the weeping copy in Máriapócs, Hungary.

(Photo courtesy of Mark Koleszar, Park Studios, G-ville, OH)

The Burton, OH , Shrine of Our Lady of Mariapoch (sic) is open on three sides. Set in a 50-acre park (donated anonymously), it is open only during the summer months.

(Photo courtesy of Mark Koleszar, Park Studios, G-ville, OH)

The original Weeping "Irish Madonna" of Győr
(Courtesy of the Diocesan Office of Győr)

The "Irish Madonna" of Győr

Location: Győr

Present-day national jurisdiction: Hungary

Name of church: Cathedral of The Assumption

Rite: Roman Catholic

Type of image: Painting of Mary adoring the sleeping Infant

Date of weeping: 1697

History: While thousands were attending Mass at Győr Cathedral on St. Patrick's day, March 17, 1697, the painting known as the "Irish Madonna" was seen to weep tears.

The picture was taken from the wall. The wall was dry, but the picture continued to shed tears, and to perspire drops of blood as well, even while it was being examined. This prodigy continued from 6 AM to 9 AM.

People of all faiths and classes hurried to see this extraordinary event. When the tears were wiped off, new drops formed, falling on the face of the Infant Jesus. Traces of these may still be seen on the picture.

A white kerchief was used to blot the tears, and was later placed in an ornate frame which is even today offered to the faithful for veneration.

A document testifying to the event was voluntarily signed by a hundred people, including the military Captain General of Győr (Count Siegebert Heister by name), the bishop, priests, Lutheran and Calvinist ministers, and even a Jewish rabbi.

But how did an "Irish Madonna" get to Hungary? It was due to Cromwell's persecution of Catholics. Cromwell invaded Ireland with 10,000 English troops in 1649, intending to eliminate all papal influence in the country. At the time, this particular picture was hanging in the cathedral of Clonfert, in the diocese of Tuam, some 25 miles north-northeast of Galway.

Bishop Walter Lynch of Clonfert was arrested and held prisoner for a time, but managed to escape. To preserve the picture from almost certain destruction, Bishop Lynch took it out of its frame, and fled with it to the continent. (The picture's frame is still in Galway.)

Bishop Lynch took refuge in Vienna, where he met János Püski, Bishop of Győr, in western Hungary. They became good friends and Bishop Püski invited Bishop Lynch to Győr, and offered to make him a member of his Cathedral Chapter, thus assuring him of an income. The Irish cleric accepted in 1655, and brought his precious picture with him.

Bishop Lynch learned the Hungarian language, and spent his income helping the poor. His charity, piety and knowledge endeared him to the inhabitants of Győr. On his deathbed, in 1663, he bequeathed his picture of the Madonna to Bishop Püski. Bishop Lynch was buried in the cathedral crypt at Győr, and his picture of the Madonna adoring the sleeping Infant was hung in

Győr Cathedral, on a side wall of St. Ann's chapel. The townspeople grew fond of it, and came to pray to the "Irish Madonna." That is where the painting was when it began to shed tears.

Following the miraculous weeping, Captain General Count Siegebert Heister had an altar erected for the miraculous image in the Cathedral's northern nave, in 1704. Later, a baroque altar replaced the first one, and the miraculous image was taken from its wooden frame and placed in a rococo silver one.

Count Heister and his wife set up a fund for the purpose of having solemn litanies and exposition of the Blessed Sacrament every Saturday, and on the vigils of the Marian feasts, at the altar in front of the miraculously weeping Madonna. The Cathedral Chapter was to administer this fund, and those funds whose establishment was inspired by the Count's example.

The "Irish Madonna" is invoked as the "Comforter of the Afflicted", and many votive offerings testify to the power of the Weeping Madonna of Győr to answer prayers. It has drawn the faithful not only from other parts of Hungary, but also from Ireland. A book of Marian shrines in Hungary, published in 1988, states that the last recorded pilgrimage from Ireland took place a century previously, in 1898, when a group of 25 Irish pilgrims visited the shrine.

On the 250th anniversary of the weeping, all the Hungarian bishops gathered at Győr. Ever since then, all the clergy of the Győr diocese make an annual pilgrimage to the shrine, combined with a day of recollection, each March 17th.

In 1967, a special Mass text honoring the Weeping Madonna was approved for use in the diocese of Győr. The following year, Pope Paul VI granted pilgrims a plenary indulgence not only for March 17th, but for every other day of the year as well, under the usual conditions.

A Marian Year was observed in 1997, to which the Holy Father sent a papal legate. On that occasion, the cathedral was raised to the rank of Minor Basilica. During his visit to Hungary in September of that year, Pope John Paul II prayed in front of the picture of the Weeping Madonna.

The basilica, whose history goes back to the time of King St. Stephen – 11th century – has two other major items of interest, both located in the Holy Trinity chapel: The first, the so-called *herma* or reliquary of the head of King St. László (Ladislaus, d.1095), which is a medieval masterpiece of the goldsmith's art. The other is the red marble sarcophagus of the martyred bishop, Blessed Vilmos Apor of Győr, who gave his life to defend women and young girls from Soviet soldiers only a short distance from the cathedral, on April 2, 1945. He was beatified in 1997.

In North America, there are two shrines of the "Irish Madonna" of Győr: at St. Anthony of Padua Church in Winnipeg, Canada, and in St. Stephen Church, in Toledo, Ohio.

The one in Toledo also has an interesting story: Archbishop Schrembs, Bishop of Toledo, visited Győr, Hungary, in 1913. He asked for a copy of the "Irish Madonna" for the Irish Catholics in his diocese. The following year, when he dedicated the new St. Stephen's Church in Toledo, he was so moved by the great sacrifices of the poor, hardworking Hungarian immigrants who had paid off almost two-thirds of the construction costs by that time, that he decided to present them with his copy of the "Irish Madonna".

In 1942, a shrine of the "Irish Madonna" was dedicated in St. Stephen's Church. Above the altar is a mosaic depicting Bishop Schrembs' presentation of the picture to the church, and below it is the actual copy brought from Hungary.

Hymn to the "Irish Madonna" of Győr

O Virgin Mother, your eyes brim with tears.
Mingled with blood, they fall upon us here.
O what great sorrow torments your pure
      heart,
Presses your tears, tears you apart.

An Irish bishop flees here in his prime.
His precious faith in Christ: his only crime.
To comfort him he brings his picture dear,
With it God does a wonder here.

The Magyars, the Irish, yours, set apart,
Their tears and their blood so wound your
      sweet heart,
Ever in prayer your lips for us pleading:
That's the secret of this weeping.

Your tears our Lord Jesus sends us herein.
May our sad nation weep over its sins!
His Sacred Heart for us His mercy shows,
Your crying people with joy overflows.

Pearls of blood, Virgin Mother, dot your
     face.
I take them as your heart's treasures of grace.
Over my sins I weep bitter tears too,
Lay them at your feet, bring them to you.

Cathedral of the Assumption of Győr, Hungary,
where the Weeping "Irish Madonna" is located.

(Photo by Erika Papp Faber)

Shrine of the Weeping "Irish Madonna" of Győr,
located in St. Stephen's Church, Toledo, OH,
with copy of the picture that had been touched to
the original. The mosaic depicts Bishop Schrembs
donating this copy to the church.

(Church-Graphic Productions, Summersville, WV)

Church of St. Stephen, Toledo, OH, where a copy
of the original Weeping "Irish Madonna" of Győr
is venerated

(Custom Studios, South Hackensack NJ)

Copy of the Weeping "Irish Madonna" of Győr in
St. Anthony of Padua Church, Winnipeg, Canada
(Photo by Ms. Sudárka Vossler)

St. Anthony of Padua Church, Winnipeg, Canada, where a copy of the Weeping "Irish Madonna" of Győr is venerated

(Photo by Ms. Sudárka Vossler)

The Weeping Madonna of Kolozsvár, originally of
Szent Miklós-Mikola

(Photo by Zágon Szentes/Szentes Zágon)

Kolozsvár

Location: originally, in Szent Miklós (Mikola); today, at Kolozsvár (Cluj-Napoca)

Present-day national jurisdiction: Romania

Name of church: Church of Szent Miklós; Piarist church of Kolozsvár

Rite: Church of Szent Miklós: Byzantine Catholic; Piarist church: Roman Catholic

Type of image: Icon – Mother and Child

Date of weeping: 1699

Original: Removed to Chapel of Szent Benedek Castle of Count Kornis;

   to the Sorrowful Mother chapel, Jesuit church in Kolozsmonostor, before Pentecost, 1699

   to the main altar, Jesuit church in Kolozsvár, a few days later

   to the large Jesuit church, 1724

Copy: for the people of Szent Miklós

Second copy: for people of Szent Benedek

History: This picture, painted by a Greek Uniate priest named Lukács in Nagyiklód (County Doboka) in 1681, was sold to a nobleman named János Kopcsa, who donated it to the Greek Uniate church at Szent Miklós, where it was placed upon the iconostasis.

On February 15, 1699, some troops of Prince Hohenzollern stationed in the area were visiting the church, and noticed that the Madonna was shedding tears. They quickly alerted the priest, who, together with representatives of the civil and military authorities, examined the picture in the presence of most of the local population.

The icon continued to weep, with some interruptions, for 26 days. It was noted that no moisture could ever be seen on the face of the Infant Jesus, only on that of Mary, and mostly on Her right eye.

Count Zsigmond Kornis had the picture removed to his castle's chapel at Szent Benedek. There, a very large crowd gathered, repenting of their sins and giving thanks to God. The weeping ceased on March 12th.

Twenty-eight witnesses gave their sworn testimony to the civil and ecclesiastic authorities, who wanted the icon removed immediately to Kolozsvár. They were opposed by Count Kornis as well as the local population, who prevailed upon them to return the icon to the church of Szent Miklós. There it was covered and sealed, and a round-the-clock guard set to prevent any tampering with the picture. This was a necessary precaution, because the *voivode* (governor) of Moldavia offered 1,000 thalers to anyone who would, by fair means or foul, obtain and bring him the weeping Madonna. Fortunately, no one made the attempt.

Permission for public veneration of the icon was given by Cardinal Leopold Kollonicz of Vienna, who directed that it be entrusted to the Jesuits of Kolozsvár. It was then temporarily transferred to the Sorrowful Mother's chapel at Kolozsmonostor, a few days before Pentecost of 1699, and then was placed with equal pomp on the main altar of the Jesuit chapel at Kolozsvár.

When the large Jesuit church was completed at Kolozsvár in 1724, the weeping icon of Szent Miklós was placed on its most ornate altar, where it has remained. Due to political machinations, the Jesuit order was temporarily dissolved in 1773, and their church was turned over to the Piarist Fathers, who administer it to this day.

Hymn to the Weeping Madonna of Kolozsvár

In Transylvania shed tears your Mikola
    image dear.
O'er the course of twenty- six days you
    mourned your sad people here.
Gain for us loyalty's virtue, at Kolozsvár's
    lovely shrine,
and for the poor Székely people, intercede,
    Mother benign.

When sorrow's arrows deeply wound, and
    I'm overcome with pain,
there's no one who would console me, and
    thus ease my lot again.
Comforter of the afflicted, for solace I run to
    you.
Come and dry my tears, dear Mother,
    Weeping Virgin Mary, do.

When above me dark clouds threaten, lashing
    lightning to and fro,
and a host of sins just tortures endlessly my
    poor soul so,
upon you I call to help me, Help of those in
    trouble too,
your protection spread over me, Weeping
    Virgin Mary, do.

When everyone looks down on me, and I lose
    all shred of hope,
sensing then the final hour, I'll be left alone
    to cope.
At that moment, my good Mother, I will
    again come to you,
help me to get up to heaven, Weeping Virgin
    Mary, do.

The Piarist (or University) Church, where the
Weeping Madonna of Kolozsvár is located.
Kolozsvár is now part of Romania.

(Photo by Zágon Szentes/Szentes Zágon)

The Weeping Madonna of Bácsfa-Szent Antal (Szentantal)

(Courtesy of Sándor and Viola Károlyi /Károlyi Sándor and Viola)

Bácsfa-Szent Antal (Szentantal)

Location: Bácsfa-Szentantal (originally spelled Szent Antal) – (Slovak: Bác)

Present-day national jurisdiction: Slovakia

Name of church: Monastery of St. Anthony of Padua

Rite: Roman Catholic

Type of image: Painting of Mother and Child

Date of weeping: 1715

History: The earliest documented mention of Bácsfa goes back to 1205. By 1238 it had a church (demolished in 1852 because of its ruined condition).

Following the devastation of the Turkish occupation, the Archbishop of Esztergom wanted to bring the Franciscan friars to the Csallóköz area. (This comprises a large island located between Pozsony and Komárom, formed by two branches of the Danube.) He therefore built, near the town of Bácsfa, a church and monastery in honor of St. Anthony of Padua, which was completed in 1677. The church became a favorite place of pilgrimage for the entire region.

Márton Liszkay, of the neighboring village of Doborgaz, made a vow in 1703 that he would have a picture painted in honor of the Blessed Mother if he were healed of his illness. In thanksgiving for a miraculous cure, he had a well-known artist from Pozsony (today known as

Bratislava) paint this picture of Mary holding the Child Jesus, and donated the painting to the church in 1705.

The painting is unusual in that Mary holds the Infant Jesus on Her right arm, and in that She wears a string of pearls around Her neck. The clothing and the facial features are also somewhat different from those usually seen in similar paintings.

On June 19, 1715, Franciscan Fr. Kelemen Jancsikovics, who had come to church at 5 o'clock in the morning to say his morning prayers, noticed that first water, then blood flowed from the Blessed Mother's eyes. This was witnessed by the other Franciscans and by the faithful.

The painting wept again between 3 AM and 4 AM on the 20th of June; at noon on the 21st; and between 4 AM and 5 AM on the 23rd of June, 1715. The tears were collected on small linen cloths, which the local people took home with them. The emperor and the bishops also received some of the tears in this fashion. A purificator (small linen cloth used during Mass), used to wipe away the tears, is still offered to the faithful for veneration.

The bishop sent a commission to examine the picture. They had it brought to one of the rooms (number 10) of the monastery, and had the room locked and sealed. In spite of the locked door, the picture returned overnight to the church, appearing on the main altar. The commission examined the lock and the seal, and found both untouched.

The following year, the Archbishop of Esztergom gave permission to display the picture for public veneration. Ever since then, the faithful have been flocking to Bácsfa to seek Our Lady's intercession.

In the Communist era, between 1950 and 1960, the monastery was used by the regime as a prison for priests.

A holy card, acquired recently, showing the Weeping Madonna of Bácsfa-Szentantal, bears the inscription: "Our weeping Mother has been watching over us for three hundred years." It also lists these "pilgrimage intentions":

"God, with His almighty love, embraces me every morning in prayer.

"At night, I give thanks together with my loved ones.

"I will not live in sin for even a moment.

"In Holy Communion, I receive the living Jesus.

"I give thanks to my Heavenly Father with my whole life.

"We will take the message, that God the Creator infinitely loves every individual, to all people.

"Jesus Christ calls every person to resurrection.

"Holy Spirit of our future, fill us with zeal for the salvation of our fellowmen."

Bácsfa-Szentantal Pilgrim's Hymn

Beautiful lily of heaven, Virgin Mary fair,
You are the ornate star of St. Anthony's church here
I have come to visit you, o choice Virgin flower,
Be so kind and hear me now, gracious Virgin Mother!

As the hind to running waters, I hastened to you,
That forgiveness for my sins I might obtain too!
I have come to visit you, o choice Virgin flower,
Conceived in St. Ann's womb, a rose-branch in a bower.

Many sinners without number you have already heard,
From the terrible fires of hell freed them like a bird.
That's why I too come to you, o choice Virgin flower,
Rose-branch who had blossomed here in a happy hour.

On your altar, like the bright sun, in splendor you
  shine,
Upon the faithful pilgrims you cast a glance benign.
Virgin Mary, look down on us, open now your ears,
See the people gathered here, listen to their pleas.

Gracious Virgin Mary, look kindly on this small band
Which in your honor traveled far, and before you
  stands,
Bringing you their offerings to lay them at your feet,
Presenting you a wreath of tears at your mercy seat.

Sinners without number have already sought you here,
Homage to your image brought, o Virgin Mother dear.
In sorrow for their sins they've shed many a tear too,
And bound them into a nice wreath, giving it to you.

The Franciscan monastery church where the
Weeping Madonna of Bácsfa-Szent Antal is located.
It is now in Slovakia.

(Courtesy of Sándor and Viola Károlyi/Károlyi Sándor and Viola)

The Weeping Madonna of Pálfalva (Sajópálfala)
which was finally returned to its original location
after 256 years.

(Photo courtesy Rev. Balázs Figecki/Figecki Balázs)

Pálfalva (Sajópálfala)

Location: (originally known as Pálfalva), Borsod-Abauj-Zemplén County

Present-day national jurisdiction: Hungary

Name of church: The Visitation

Rite: Byzantine Catholic

Type of image: Painting of Mother and Child with crowns

Date of weeping: 1717

Original: Taken to Eger;

disappeared in 1950;

returned to Sajópálfala in 1973

Copy: Made in 1927, and placed in the church of Sajópálfala

History: The first documentary mention of Pálfalva occurred in 1320, in a property deed of an inheritance. The town was destroyed during the Turkish occupation, and resettled by Byzantine Catholics of Rusyn ethnicity. The oldest Byzantine Catholic hymnal in Hungary (*Irmologion*) was copied by hand in Pálfalva in 1755, and is unique in its melodies which, though modified through the use of Hungarian, can still be found in Byzantine liturgical music in Hungary.

From January 6 to February 16, 1717, the painting of the Madonna and Child in the Byzantine Catholic church was seen to perspire and shed tears. When Father Péter Lipmizky (or Lipniczki), the Pastor, first saw them, he gave a stirring homily, urging the faithful to do penance, so that many of the onlookers were moved to heartfelt sorrow for their sins.

The phenomena of the perspiration and shedding of tears was witnessed by many, and 17 people testified under oath to their authenticity. (The descendents of many of the witnesses still reside in Sajópálfala to this day.) Brown or dark red tears were visible on both the right and left eyes of the picture. They neither froze in the bitter cold weather, nor did they dry up from the heat of the stove near the picture. The examining Vicar General testified that, taking a teardrop with a knife, he found it to be a true dark bloody drop. When he tried to wipe the perspiration from the picture's forehead with a small linen cloth, he was unable to do so, as new drops kept forming all the time.

The Bishop ordered the weeping picture to be brought to Eger, where, after examination by Church authorities, it was placed in the Franciscan church. (According to the custom of pilgrimage shrines at the time, the picture, painted on canvas by an unknown early 18th century artist, was then decorated with crowns, for both Mary and the Infant Jesus.)

But the people of Pálfalva remembered, passing on the information about their miraculous picture's whereabouts from father to son. Every year in the fall, on the feast of Our Lady of Sorrows, they went on pilgrimage to their picture in Eger, and kept asking for its return.

But the picture was not returned, and so they finally had a copy made, in 1927. This copy was placed in the church at Sajópálfala with great ceremony. Pilgrims began to visit their copy of the weeping Madonna. Unfortunately, the pastor was transferred two years later. Pilgrims still came for a while, but World War II put an end to pilgrimages. The people of Sajópálfala, however, continued their pilgrimages to Eger to seek out their original miraculous picture.

In 1950, all the monasteries in Hungary were closed by the Communists, and the religious orders were disbanded. Now, when the people of Sajópálfala went on pilgrimage to Eger, they no longer found their treasure, the miraculously weeping picture. Inquiries concerning its whereabouts went unanswered.

Years went by. A new pastor, Father Balázs Figeczki, was assigned to the town in 1965. Finding the miraculously weeping Madonna was first among the requests presented to him by the congregation. They looked for it in Eger as well as in Esztergom, the primatial see, but without success.

Then, in 1969, a Franciscan was assigned as Pastor to a nearby town, and he tipped off Pastor Figeczki to look for the picture in the church of Pécsürög, in the diocese of Pécs in the south of Hungary. In the spirit of fraternal charity, he informed him that a Franciscan had taken the miraculously weeping picture there at the time of the dissolution of the religious orders.

A delegation went to investigate, and to their great joy found the picture to have been placed over the main altar. The Pastor of Pécsürög explained that it was the original Weeping Madonna of Sajópálfala.

Permission for its return had to be obtained from three dioceses: that of Eger, where the picture had originally been; of Pécs, where it was found; and of Hajdudorog, which administers the Byzantine rite.

All this took time, and it was not until October 1973 that the miraculously weeping Madonna of Sajópálfala could return to its place of origin. Its return was greeted with great joy.

The faithful surround the picture with great devotion and love. They pray before it for the sick, for young men who have been drafted into the army, for students and for every good intention.

The copy has been placed on a side wall of the sanctuary.

The church's official annual days of Marian pilgrimage are Pentecost Sunday, and the third Sunday of October, commemorating the picture's return.

Every June, on the Monday following the last day of school, the youth of the area, some 200-300 strong, together with 15-20 priests, gather at Sajópálfala in thanksgiving for the past school year.

It was the oral tradition of the people of Sajópálfala and of the Franciscans that eventually led to the return of this miraculous picture to its original church, 256 years after it was taken away! Truly a remarkable story, a story of adventure, perseverance and devotion!

Prayer to Our Lady of Pálfalva

Our Lady of Pálfalva, kindly protecting, motherly hand! Reward thy pious faithful, who have recourse to Thee, for our constantly blossoming love. Before this picture, together with thousands of the faithful, we adore the divine Majesty with the great veneration of the Mother of God, whom we beg not to cease interceding for us sinners, in our great need. Amen.

(from 1863)

Copy of the Weeping Madonna of Pálfalva
(Sajópálfala), now on the side wall of the sanctuary
(Courtesy Rev. Balázs Figecki/Figecki Balázs)

Church of Sajópálfala, now housing both the
original and the copy of the Weeping Madonna
(Courtesy Rev. Balázs Figecki/Figecki Balázs)

The "Weeping Madonna" invoked at Baja-
Máriakönnye. There is no documented evidence
that this painting ever shed tears. Devotion here is
based merely on legend.

(Photo József Kerekes/Kerekes József, courtesy Rev. Mátyás
Schindler/Schindler Mátyás)

Baja-Máriakönnye

Location: Near Baja, Bács-Kiskun County; Slavonic name: Vodica

Present-day national jurisdiction: Hungary

Name of church: Nativity of Our Lady

Rite: Roman Catholic and Byzantine Catholic

Type of image: Painting of Mother and Child with crowns

Date of weeping: No historic record

History: Historic sources concerning this shrine mention only that religious devotion developed around the two holy springs in the 18th century. It seems a farm overseer was traveling with his family when the carriage overturned near the springs, but no one was injured. In gratitude for his family's escape, he had a chapel built near the springs, and placed in it a copy of the picture of Our Lady of Prompt Succor. Pilgrims flocked to the chapel in great numbers, and many prayers were answered there. It was officially declared a shrine by Pope Pius VII, who granted indulgences to the pilgrims in 1817.

The area is near the border with present-day Serbia, and is inhabited by Hungarians as well as Serbs. Each ethnic group has is own legend about the origin of the shrine. The Hungarian legend tells of a picture of Our Lady which used to hang on a tree here. A wanderer stopped to rest at the foot of the tree, and was bemoaning his sad fate, when drops of water fell on his arms, although it was not raining. He looked up, and saw tears flow from the Blessed Virgin's eyes. She told him to draw water from the spring. Not seeing one, the wanderer looked around, and noticed that Our Lady's tears were turning into a spring.

The Serb legend tells of two students, one a Hungarian, the other a Serb, being attacked by wolves. In mortal danger, they noticed a picture of Our Lady high on a tree. They prayed to Her for help, and were saved. Later, they found two springs under the tree. They vowed to dedicate this place to Our Lady, each according to his own rite.

Ever since then, Roman and Byzantine Catholics have gathered for their devotions around the two springs. It is visited not only by Hungarians, but also by Catholic Serbs, Slovaks, Germans and a Slavonic ethnic group known as "Sokác". When the newly renovated chapel was dedicated in 1973 by the Archbishop of Kalocsa, he gave his homily in Hungarian, Serbo-Croatian and German.

Despite its name ("Mária könnye" means "Mary's tears"), there is no documentation of an actual weeping of the picture at this shrine. But with or without tears, She demonstrates in this place that She is Mother of us all.

✼

There is no record of any hymn associated specifically with the shrine of Baja-Máriakönnye.

The chapel where the so-called "Weeping Madonna" of Baja-Máriakönnye is located.
(Photo József Kerekes/Kerekes József, courtesy Rev. Mátyás Schindler/Schindler Mátyás)

Tears, Blood and Sweat

In all but one of the Weeping Madonnas of historic Hungary (the painting at *Nagyszombat*), Jesus was also depicted in some way. Yet it was always *MARY* who wept, not Jesus.

What could have been the reason? Perhaps Our Lady wanted to indicate that Her motherly heart was moved. But why do mothers cry?

    a) for joy
    b) over children who are hurt
    c) for children who go astray
    d) to grieve over a death

How can these causes be applied to the ten Weeping Madonnas of Historic Hungary?

Joy – at *Klokocsó* over the "Union of Ungvár"; and at *Baja-Máriakönnye*, presumably over the future gathering of Her children of different rites at that shrine.

All the other reasons can be applied to the other eight instances of weeping. (Some Carpatho-Rusyns also interpret the *Klokocsó* weeping as a sign of Mary's sorrow over their fate of religious discrimination, as well as their living in conditions of great poverty and political oppression.)

✣

While all ten paintings of Mary wept tears (although one "weeping", that of Baja-Máriakönnye, is only a legend), a few also perspired (sweated), and some wept tears of blood. Here's the breakdown:

Bloody tears: 2 :
    Bácsfa-Szent Antal – 1715
    Pálfalva – 1717

Plain sweat: 3 :
    Királyfalva: Mary wept, Jesus sweated – 1683
    Nagyszombat: Mary wept and sweated – 1708
    Pálfalva – Mary wept bloody tears and sweated – 1717

Sweated blood: 1 :
    Győr – Mary wept and sweated blood – 1697

⁕

What may be the significance of *bloody tears*?

We know from Scripture that blood was believed to reconcile man to God, to seal a covenant and to create the most intimate relationship between the parties to an agreement. Bloody tears, then, might signify both sorrow and reconciliation, sealed with Mary's bloody tears.

⁕

And perspiration (sweat)? From the time Adam was driven from Eden (Gn 3:19), "the sweat of your brow" has indicated heavy labor. So when the body of Jesus sweated in the arms of His weeping Mother *(Királyfalva)*, or Mary sweated blood as Her tears were falling in *Győr*, we can surmise that these were signs of the great effort, anguish and suffering we caused Jesus and Mary. (Just recall Jesus' agony in the Garden of Gethsemane, Lk 22:44).

An Attempt at Analysis

Before attempting to analyze the phenomena of these ten Weeping Madonnas in historic Hungary, it would be helpful to take a look at the events leading up to the time when these images began to weep (and some, to sweat). Many could be linked to the political situation at the time, which was dominated by Turkish rule and the struggle against the Turks.

Following the Protestant Revolt, much of Hungary went over to the Lutheran and Calvinist faiths. Almost simultaneously, the Turks renewed their attacks, which had been intermittent for several centuries. In 1526, they thoroughly defeated the Hungarian forces at the battle of Mohács, killing the king and most of the nobility, thereby depriving the country of political leadership. This marked the beginning of 160 years of Turkish rule.

Those, who were not killed outright, were in constant fear of their lives. Many went into hiding in the thick forests that still existed in those days, or in swampy areas. Their houses and churches were burnt, their produce and livestock either destroyed or confiscated. Hunger and poverty and fear made up the reality of life for the people of Hungary under Turkish rule. The population was decimated, so much so, that large-scale re-population with foreign settlers was undertaken once the Turks had been driven from the land.

Although the Austrian Hapsburgs helped to fight against the Turks, they ruled the western part of historic

Hungary. The emperor, particularly Leopold I, tried with all his might to force absolutist rule upon the whole country. His general, Montecuccoli, retreated from the Turks all across Hungary, finally being forced to fight at Szentgotthárd, at the Austrian frontier. The Christian forces won a major victory over the Turks there, but Montecuccoli failed to follow up: he did not pursue the enemy.

Infinitely worse, however, was the hasty and shameful peace treaty concluded by the Austrians with the Turks at Vasvár (1664), which left all the occupied territories, including Transylvania, in Turkish hands for 20 years, and even went so far as to make a "present" of 200,000 *talers* to the Sultan! It gave the impression that not the Christians, but the Turks had won! The Hungarian people felt totally betrayed.

Even the Catholic supporters of the Hapsburgs turned against them, and a political conspiracy to conclude a French alliance seemed a viable solution. However, it was discovered, and gave the Austrians an excuse to suspend the constitution and impose absolutist rule. Unprecedented political oppression followed, bringing about the moral and material destruction of the Hungarians. The Protestants suffered most, with many of their ministers being sent to the galleys by the Austrians.

Thousands took up guerrilla warfare against Austrian troops, styling themselves "kurucok", a new type of "crusaders". Because of their efforts, some Protestants were allowed to practice their religion again, in certain localities, and the constitution was re-established by the emperor.

When the Turks laid siege to Vienna in 1683, the Christian forces of Europe finally rallied against the Muslim threat. Led by the Polish king John Sobieski, they won a complete victory. This was the beginning of a 16-year long war of liberation from Turkish rule. Buda was recaptured from the Turks in 1686. The victory of Zenta in 1697 by Prince Eugene of Savoy marked a major defeat of the Turks in Hungary, although the last Turks were not driven out until 1718.

*

The first weeping of the picture of *Nagyszombat* in 1663 occurred just before the bloody battle of Párkány. In that year, fighting broke out between the Turks and Austrians, and Hungarians saw their chance. Miklós Zrinyi attacked the Turks with his own troops, freed the Csallóköz area and dealt several blows on the Turkish forces. The "Weeping Virgin of Nagyszombat" saved the city from Turkish attack by having a thick fog settle on the city.

The next "Weeping Virgin" was that of *Királyfalva*, which shed its tears in 1683, while the dead body of Jesus in Her lap was covered with perspiration. It was in that year that the Turks were driven from Vienna by the combined European forces under John Sobieski, and the town, together with Pozsony (known today as Bratislava), was threatened by the Turks.

The first weeping of the *Máriapócs* icon took place at the end of 1696. The following year, because of the political and economic oppression of the Hapsburgs, a revolt led by Francis Rákóczi II broke out in Upper Hungary, against "the barbarous usage they show both in religious and civil matters," as described by England's minister to Vienna. It was an effort to get rid of foreign oppression, and Slovaks, Ruthenians and other mountain folk joined the Hungarians in opposing the Hapsburgs. According to Jordánszky, "The condition of our dear homeland was indeed lamentable then, on account of internal riots..."

Unfortunately, the French help Rákóczi hoped for did not materialize, and his insurrection suffered several major defeats, one in 1708 and another in 1710. The plague was also rampant at the time, and people were in great anguish. Was it a coincidence then that the "Weeping Madonna" of *Nagyszombat* shed tears, for the second time, in 1708?

Meanwhile, the "Weeping Madonna" of *Kolozsvár* had shed tears in 1699, the year Austria gained control over Hungary and Transylvania. The people interpreted this prodigy at the time as "the Mother of Mercy interceding for us with Her Son, with tears."

The last weeping that could be related to the Turkish times in Hungary was the one at *Pálfalva.* It occurred in 1717, the year Eugene of Savoy recaptured Nándorfehérvár (known today as Belgrade), and finally liberated the last piece of Hungarian territory from the Muslims.

※

The *"Irish Madonna" of Győr* wept in 1697. As mentioned above, that was the year of Rákóczi's revolt, as well as the victory over the Turks at Zenta. Yet this incident of weeping was perhaps more of an "international" event, also referring to events in the painting's place of origin, because it occurred at the time that persecution of Catholics in Ireland was renewed. In that year, Parliament ordered the expulsion of all priests from Ireland. A Protestant national church was established, and only members of this national church could preside at funerals. Oppression and poverty characterized both Ireland and Hungary at that time. There were plenty of reasons for Mary to shed tears!

✻

Two main rites, the Byzantine Catholic and the Roman Catholic, had existed in historic Hungary side by side, although the Roman rite was more widespread, being followed by the successors of St. Stephen, the first king. Over the centuries, the Byzantines came to feel that they were discriminated against, treated as second-class citizens within the Church, although both Byzantine and Roman Catholics suffered equally at the hands of the Turks.

To bridge this gap among the two rites, a movement towards reconciliation slowly grew in momentum, until it reached its culmination in the "Union of Ungvár" (now Uzhgorod) in 1646. This brought about a revitalized union of Byzantine rite Catholics with Roman Catholics.

Consequently, the weeping of the icon at the Byzantine Catholic Church at *Klokocsó* was regarded by some as a sign from heaven, a recognition of all their sufferings, but also a sign of joy, thinking that Mary shed tears of happiness over their efforts at revitalizing their union with the Apostolic See.

✻

The weeping of the Marian paintings brought about repentance of the populace. This is mentioned especially in the early historic description of Marian shrines written by Elek Jordánszky in 1836, about the following:

Királyfalva (1683) : the chapel has become a place of pilgrimage for the people of the surrounding area, where "those who come to beg the divine mercy in front of this picture, are frequently consoled through the intercession of the Mother of Mercy."

Győr (1697) : "Some (on seeing the prodigy) began to weep and mourn their sins." A foundation was established by Count Heister for the exposition of the Blessed Sacrament, the recitation of litanies on certain days, and the celebration of Mass at certain times, before the Weeping Madonna.

Kolozsvár (1699): "An innumerable crowd, made up of every class of society, gathered. Most of them examined themselves, and repented of their sins; they also gave thanks to the merciful God, who deigned to provide such a powerful Advocate for our pitiable country, and to warn us with the shedding of tears."

Nagyszombat (1708): people were "deeply touched, and very many did penance, and with contrite heart decried their former deviation from the law of God, being convinced that such bitter distress befalls us on account of our sins, which are worthy even of the merciful tears of the Mother of God."

Pálfalva (1717) : The weeping prompted the Pastor to give a stirring homily, "urging the faithful to do penance, so that many who saw the blood-like sweat and weeping were moved to heartfelt fear of God and sorrow for their sins."

✽

The *second weeping* of the *Máriapócs copy* occurred in 1905, not long after divorce was legalized in Hungary. This one needs no analysis!

Looking at the longer term, however, we might also conjecture that this time Our Lady was weeping over the tremendous suffering that was soon to be inflicted on the Hungarian people by World War I and its aftermath. For it occurred only nine years before the outbreak of hostilities, and 15 years before the dismemberment of historic Hungary, when two-thirds of the country's territory was lopped off to help create the countries of Czechoslovakia and Yugoslavia and to add Transylvania to Romania. With the Treaty of Trianon, some 5 million Hungarians became minorities overnight, treated as enemy aliens in their own country, in the land of their forefathers.

Yes, Our Lady had good reason to cry!

✽

The Treaty of Trianon put six of the ten Weeping Madonnas outside the borders of historic Hungary. Today, only the *second* icon of *Máriapócs*, the "Irish Madonna" of *Győr*, the icon of *Pálfalva* and the ecumenically honored Madonna of *Baja-Máriakönnye* are left within the borders of truncated Hungary.

✽

Yet when all is said and done, "who can discern what the Lord wills?" (Ws 9:13b) As finite creatures, we can only guess at His purposes. Since everything He does has a reason, and since He does not perform miracles frivolously, these extraordinary events, such as the weeping of paintings, must also have a purpose.

Although we don't know the mind of God, we do know that He loves us and wills that all of us, His children, reach the infinite happiness of seeing Him for eternity. In some way, then, these Weeping Madonnas also have their place in this overall plan of God. Through the intercession of Mary, may they help us to achieve our goal of the Beatific Vision!

Our Lady of Tears, please pray for us all! Amen.

✣

Meditation

"My tears are stored in your flask" says Psalm 56:9. Because we are precious in the sight of the Lord, so are our tears, and He wishes to save them. He notes our sorrows and remembers them.

If this verse applies to us, how much more does it apply to Mary! For Mary is the one created being who has been sinless from the moment of Her conception, and whose will conforms perfectly to God's will. How much more pleasing to Him is Her every action! How much more will He note Mary's sorrows, and remember them!

And so this verse from Psalm 56 leads us to believe that God has also stored up in His flask Mary's tears, shed in nine places in Hungary, remembering their cause and treasuring Her sorrow. Can He then ever forget the troubles of the Hungarian people? Or ever forsake them? Mary's tears are a pledge of God's Providence for His Hungarian children!

Thank You, Lord! Thank you, Blessed Mother, *Magyarok Nagyasszonya*, Great Lady of the Hungarians! Thank you, for drawing God's special attention to our plight over the years by shedding your precious tears on our behalf!

May we never again give you cause to cry for our sins, and may the Lord preserve us from external evils like those which moved you to tears in the past!

Our Weeping Virgin Mother, please continue to keep us, your special heritage, in your loving care. Amen.

✼

Hungarian Texts of the Hymns and Prayers Used

1) Hymn to the Weeping Madonna of Nagyszombat *

Köszöntésre jöttünk Szűz Máriához,
Drága könnyét ontó égi Anyánkhoz!
Lelkünk tárva igaz áhitattal,
Ajkunk dallal, öröm-hódolattal.

Jó Anyánk, hálánk zeng ebben a dalban,
Amiért fáj néked a világ baja,
Mert az emberszívekben sok a jaj,
Melyre enyhet csak szent szíved adhat.

Vajúdó korunknak gyötrelme tör ránk,
Irigység s gyűlölet lelkünket rontják,
Szívünk szorong, milyen lesz a holnap?
Drága könnyed az egyetlen vigasz.

Szent Fiad meghalt a kereszten értünk,
A poklok láncait széttörte nékünk,
Zúzzuk mi is rossz hajlamunk s vétkünk,
S szabad szívvel szárnyal föl majd hitünk.

Könnyező Szűzanyánk, tanits meg kérünk,
Másért ne sírjunk csak, ha sok a vétkünk.
Rettegni sem kell viharos éjben,
Ha bízunk Szíved s Fiad Szívében.

Győzünk a harcban, hisz velünk az Isten,
És ereje oly nagy vérnek és könnynek,
Te és Jézus sorsunk osztályrésze,
Együtt győzünk földön e szent hitben.

Drága könnyed, szent Szűz, üzeni nékünk,
Csókoljuk meg végre súlyos keresztünk.
Búcsuszóra földre borul térdünk,
Fogadd szent Szűz gyermeki hűségünk.

* N.B. This same hymn, with minor variations, and in a smoother poetic form, has also been published as referring to the *Weeping Madonna of Győr.*

2) Prayer to Our Lady of Máriapócs

Könnyező Szűz Anyám, bűnösök menedéke, könnyeidre kérlek, eszközöld ki Jézusnál bűneim bocsánatát, nyerd meg számomra és enyéimre szent Fiad áldását. Enyhítsd szenvedéseinket, gyógyítsd meg betegségeinket, vigasztalj szomorúságunkban, segíts az erényes életbe, vezess végül a boldog mennyországba!

Ó könnyező Szűz, ó drága Istenanya, emlékezzél meg rólunk Jézusnál, most és halálunk óráján. Ámen.

3) Máriapócs Pilgrims' Hymn

Isten hozott e szent helyre, ájtatos buzgó
        hívek,
Hol az édes jó Szűzanya örömmel vár titeket.

Refrain:

Szűz Mária, egek gyöngye, add áldásod
híveidre,
Drágalátós kezeiddel ölelj minket
szívedre.

Itt a pócsi szép templomban osztja dúsan
áldását,
Kinek szíve igaz s tiszta, meghallgatja
fohászát.
Refrain

Vedd kedvesen égi anyánk ezen búcsú-
járásunk,
Melyet most e szent helyeden neked itt
felajánlunk.
Refrain

**4) Hymn to the Weeping Madonna of Győr
(the "Irish Madonna")**

Könnyes a két szemed, ó Szűzanyánk.
Véresen csordul a könnye reánk.
Jaj, milyen bánat gyötri szívedet,
Sajtolja ki könnyeidet.

Futva fut írhoni püspök ide;
bűne csak krisztusi drága hite.
Képedet hozza édes vigaszul,
Itt tesz csodát véle az Úr.

Két kicsi nép, magyar, ír a Tied,
Könnyük is, vérük is vérzi szíved.
Ajkadat értünk imára nyitod.
Ezt súgja e drága titok.

Könnyedet Jézusunk küldi nekünk,
Sírjon a vétkein bús nemzetünk!
Szent Szíve rajtunk megint könyörül,
Síró néped újra örül.

Vérgyöngy a képeden, ó Szűzanyánk!
Fölszedem hű szíved kincse gyanánt.
Bűnömet én is könnyel siratom:
Lábad elé mind lerakom.

5) Hymn to the Weeping Madonna of Kolozsvár (Mikola)

Mikolai drága képed Erdély földjén
    könnyezett.
Huszonhat napon keresztül sirattad bús
    népedet.
Nyerd meg a hűség erényét, Kolozsvár szép
    kegyhelyén,
És könyörögj most is, Anyánk, szegény
    székely népedért.

Ha a bánat nyila sebez és elönt a fájdalom,
Nincsen aki vigasztaljon, és könnyítsen
    sorsomon.
Enyhületért hozzád futok, szomorúak
    Vigasza,

Száritsd föl a könnyeimet, Könnyező Szűz
Mária.

Ha fölöttem sötét felhő villámait csapdossa,
Lelkemet a vétkek hada szüntelenül kínozza,
Segítségül téged hívlak, bajbanlévők
Gyámola,
Oltalmadat terjeszd fölém, Könnyező Szűz
Mária.

Ha mindenki megvet engem, s reményemet
elvesztem,
Érezve a végső órát, nem lesz senki
mellettem.
Végpercemben hozzád jövök, te igazi jó
Anya,
Segíts engem föl a mennybe, Könnyező Szűz
Mária.

6) Hymn to the Weeping Madonna of Bácsfa-Szentantal

Óh, egeknek lilioma, szép szűz Mária,
Szentantali templomnak ékes csillaga!
Én Tehozzád idejöttem ékes szűz virág.
Máltóztassál meghallgatni kegyes szűz
Anyánk!

Mint a szarvas kútforráshoz, hozzád siettem!
Bűneimnek bocsánatát hogy megnyerhessem.
Én Tehozzád jöttem ékes szűz virág!
Szent Anna asszony méhében oltott rózsaág.

Sok számtalan bűnösöket már meghallgattál,
A pokolnak nagy tüzéből szabadítottál.
Én is azért hozzád jöttem, ékes szűz virág,
E gyönyörű kegyhelyen kinyílt rózsaág.

Mint fényes nap, oltárodon akként
    tündöklesz,
Az ide zarándoklókra le is tekintesz.
Tekints reánk szűz Mária, nyisd meg füleid.
Hallgasd meg itt egybegyűlt nép
    könyörgéseit.

Nézz le kegyes szűz Mária a kis seregre,
Mely messze földről utazott tiszteletedre,
Hogy Te néked ajándékot bőven oszthasson,
Egy könnyből kötött koszorút átadhasson.

Sok számtalan nagy bűnös már itt
    megkeresett,
Szűz anyai képed előtt áldozatot tett.
Bűnei bocsánatáért könnyet hullatott,
Abból font egy szép koszorút, mit neked
    adott.

7) Prayer to the Weeping Madonna of Pálfalva

Pálfalvai Boldogasszony! Jóságos, oltalmazó,
anyai kéz! Jutalmazd meg Érted állandóan
fakadó szeretetünkért a Tehozzád járó buzgó
híveidet. Ezer hívőkkel e kép előtt imádjuk a
felséges Istent az Istenanya nagy tiszteletével,
kitől kérjük, hogy ne szünjön esedezni érettünk
bűnösökért, a mi nagy ínségeinkben. Ámen.

Bibliography

A bécsi Szent István-dóm és magyar emlékei. *(St. Stephen's Cathedral of Vienna and its Hungarian Relics). (Booklet)* Rev. István Cser-Palkovits, SJ, Sankt Stephan Verein, Wien, 1984.

A Győri Szüzanya kegyképének története. *(The Story of the Miraculous Picture of the Virgin Mother of Győr). (Booklet)* St. Anthony of Padua Church, Winnipeg, Canada.

A Könnyező Máriapócsi Szűzanya csodatevő kegyképe. *(The Wonder-working Picture of the Weeping Virgin Mother of Máriapócs).* (Booklet) Dr. Bacsóka Pál, photos by Erdős Miklós. Örökségünk Kiadó.

Der Dom zu Wiener Neustadt. *(The Cathedral of Wiener Neustadt)* A guidebook to the cathedral.

Holy card from Máriapócs.

Holy card from Szentantal-Bács.

"Hungarians Gather to Honor Mary", article on Máriapócs in ONE, May 2005, published by Catholic Near East Welfare Association.

Magyarország Szűz Mária kegyhelyei: Búcsújárók könyve. *(Marian Shrines in Hungary: A Book for Pilgrims).* Szenthelyi-Molnár István and Mauks Márta. Szent István Társulat. Budapest, 1988.

Magyar Országban, 's az ahoz tartozó Részekben lévő bóldogságos Szűz Mária kegyelem' Képeinek rövid

leírása. *(A Brief Description of the Miraculous Marian Pictures Located in Hungary and in the Areas Belonging to It)*. Jordánszky Elek. Fakszimile kiadás. Akadémiai Kiadó. 1988. (Originally published in 1836, it was reissued in a facsimile edition in 1988.)

Magyar zarándokhelyek V. 1990. *(Hungarian Places of Pilgrimage V)*. (Calendar)

Mária kegyhelyek Mária országában. *(Marian Shrines in Mary's Land)*. Ipolyvölgyi Németh Krizosztom. Moczár Béla. 1998.

Mariapoch: Shrine of Mary's Compassion. The story of this miraculous weeping icon and the shrine in Burton, Ohio, named in its honor. Video. Gemini Productions.

Novena in Honor of Madonna of Ireland. St. Stephen's Church, Toledo, Ohio. (Booklet)

Sajópálfala. 1717-1950-1973-1998. (Leaflet)

The Shrine of Our Weeping Mother of Máriapócs and the Mission of the Basilian Fathers of Máriapócs. Stephen J. Skinta, O.S.B.M. 1973.

The Weeping Icon of Mariapovch on the 300th Anniversary of the First Miraculous Weeping. Downloaded from Internet website Carpatho-Rusyn Spirituality.

Történelmi zarándokhelyek VI. 1991. *(Historic Places of Pilgrimage)* (Calendar)

The Weeping Icon of Klokochovo. Downloaded from Internet website: www.carpatho-rusyn.org/spirit/kloko.htm.

Zarándokok könyve. *(The Pilgrims' Book).* Berecz Sándor, plébános, Római katolikus plébánia hivatal, YU 24415 Backi Vinogradi, Beogradska 23. 1986.

Web page: www.búcsújárás.hu

Addendum

Statue of Our Lady of Fatima, clearly weeping oil, in the cemetery of Jánoshida

(Photo by Károly Kósa/Kósa Károly)

Jánoshida

Location: On the banks of the Zagyva, in the diocese of Eger, between Jászberény and Szolnok

Present-day national jurisdiction: Hungary

Type of image: Statue of Our Lady of Fatima, located in Jánoshida cemetery over the grave of former Pastor, Rev. Albert Sebestyén

Date of first weeping: March 15, 2003

History: Fr. Albert Sebestyén, Pastor of Jánoshida, had a great devotion to Our Lady, and was able to deepen that devotion among his parishioners in the 35 years he served there. He died in September 2000, and was buried in the local cemetery.

The following month, October 2000, villagers traveled to Fatima on pilgrimage. Among them was a young man from the neighboring village, who bought a statue of Our Lady of Fatima and, on his return, placed it on Fr. Sebestyén's grave. Later on, the statue was brought into the church and placed at the edge of the altar, where it remained for a year.

The parishioners built a small niche between the Pastor's grave and the grave of the Norbertine Provincial who died in 1985. On September 13th, 2001, they placed the statue in the niche. They put a sheet of glass over the front of the niche, held in place by a wooden frame. Thus the statue cannot be touched, unless the covering is forcibly removed. The sacristan and many of the faithful often went to pray there.

On March 15th, 2003, on the day Hungarians commemorate the freedom fight of 1848 against the Austrians, the people praying in the cemetery noticed a yellow fluid flowing in a wide streak from the statue's right eye. This fluid did not disappear or evaporate, but seems to have solidified.

On July 13th, the faithful noted the appearance of transparent tears as well, and the lower eyelid seemed to be somewhat swollen.

On October 13th, more fluid flowed from Mary's eye, and the lower eyelid was considerably swollen. At the same time, people noticed that the yellow coloring under the eyelid was now starting under the left eye too, and a transparent-seeming teardrop also appeared.

Photographs were taken of the events, both of March 15th and October 13th, on which the lasting tears can be plainly seen. Some cures have already been noted. Groups of pilgrims now visit the Jánoshida cemetery, especially on the anniversaries of Mary's apparitions at Fatima.

A visionary named Katalin and her sister, during one of their visits to the cemetery, noticed that Mary's eye, which had been very swollen when they arrived, lost its swollen look, and they could see Her glance. She reported that Mary told her: "Thank you for coming to me. You have lessened my pain, because you have prayed here. I am crying on account of my priests! Speak about me! They make light of me! Send people to me! Let those who have many worries, many problems, come here. Let them pray to me, I will help them! I wait for everyone, so that they might come and pray to me. I await not only Catholics, but let everyone come to me!"

Lest people misunderstand, Mary also said: "You serve my Son first, then me."

On another visit, when they were still far away from the statue and could not see it yet because of the crowd, Katalin heard Our Lady say: "My tears have lessened. You have prayed so much, but it's not enough!"

Mary also told a visionary named Ilona (who also has the stigmata): "The face of the Marian statue at Jánoshida has tears of oil – for the sake of permanence – which, together with the original tears, have solidified on the chin." Ilona says that by Her tears, the Blessed Virgin urges humanity to convert and do penance.

Another visionary, Rózsika Marián of Seuca (Szőkefalva), Romania, who received messages from Our Lady for 10 years, asked her about the "picture" of Jánoshida when She appeared to her on February 26th, 2004. Our Lady corrected her, saying, "My daughter, that's a statue, not a picture. **They are the tears of my light.**"

Then on June 17, 2005, when Our Lady appeared to Rózsika in Seuca (Szőkefalva), Romania, for the last time (as She had foretold), She said, "My name here, in this place, is '**The Queen of Light**'." (The 120 concelebrating priests and the 30,000 faithful who had gathered for Mary's last message in this place saw a miracle of the sun reminiscent of the one at Fatima.)

On December 2, 2004, Our Lady appeared to the seer Mirjana in her monthly apparition in Medjugorje.

Although she has never transmitted the messages she receives on the 2nd of each month, this time Mirjana wrote down Our Lady's message and asked that it be translated for the pilgrims who were there. Surprisingly, in this message, Mary asked for help, for the same purpose as She asked at Jánoshida – for reconciliation, conversion of unbelievers. She said to Mirjana: "I need you! I'm calling you, I seek your help! Reconcile with yourself, with God and with your neighbor. In this way you'll help me. Convert the non-believers! **Remove the tears from my face!**"

Although Jánoshida has been added to a Hungarian pilgrims' website, there has been no report so far of an examination by Church authorities. The current Pastor, who comes from a neighboring village to minister to the faithful at Jánoshida, has even forbidden the sale of photographs of the weeping statue. For the Church does not rush headlong into approving apparitions or devotions. Historically, Church authorities have, at first, usually been very cautious or even downright hostile to any reported phenomena.

But if the tears of Jánoshida ARE authentic, Mary will see to it that the truth is brought to light!

✳

Niche of the so-called Weeping Madonna of
Jánoshida, with monument of the former Pastor,
Fr. Albert Sebestyén

(Photo by Judit Juhász/Juhász Judit)

Statue of Our Lady of Fatima, with redness around the right eye, in the cemetery at Jánoshida

(Photo by Judit Juhász/Juhász Judit)

Sources of Jánoshida Information

Internet:

"Búcsújárás honlapja" (Hungarian pilgrimage home page)

E-mail response by Dennis Nolan of www.childrenofmedjugorje

"Jánoshida honlap" (Hungarian home page for Jánoshida) – also source for close-up photo

"Zarándok honlap" (Hungarian pilgrim home page)

Personal correspondence of Pál Vincze/Vincze Pál

About the Author

Erika Papp Faber was born in Hungary, but has lived in the United States since her childhood. She taught Hungarian at the New York Saturday School, where she also served as Principal. More recently, she has taught Hungarian at Magyar Studies of America in Fairfield, CT, where she was also Principal.

Among her published works are numerous articles on Hungarian and religious subjects, both in English and Hungarian. Previous booklets include "Keeping Our Eyes Fixed on HIM: reflections on Gospel events by a lay Catholic"; "God Sustains Widows: a scriptural view"; "Who Wants to be an Artichoke?" (poems); and "A csipkebokorból" (Hungarian poems).

She has compiled an anthology of Hungarian poetry, which she has translated, and which awaits a publisher. She has also written a booklet of reflections on the Rosary, which awaits a publisher.

In addition to Hungarian, Erika Papp Faber has translated articles from German, French, Italian, Spanish and Portuguese. A book from the French, and another from the German, was published by Orbis Books.

Erika Papp Faber holds a degree in Foreign Service from Georgetown University.

All Generations Shall Call Me Blessed *by Fr. Stefano Manelli, F.I.* A scholarly, easy to read book tracing Mary's role in the Old Testament through prophecies, figures, and symbols to Mary's presence in the New Testament. A concise exposition which shows clearly Mary's place in the economy of Salvation.

Totus Tuus *by Msgr. Arthur Burton Calkins* provides a thorough examination of the Holy Father's thoughts on total consecration or entrustment to Our Lady based on the historic, theological and scriptural evidence. Vital in clearing away some misunderstandings about entrustment and consecration.

Jesus Our Eucharistic Love *by Fr. Stefano Manelli, F.I.* A treasure of Eucharistic devotional writings and examples from the Saints showing their stirring Eucharistic love and devotion. A valuable aid for reading meditatively before the Blessed Sacrament.

Virgo Facta Ecclesia *by Franciscan Friars of the Immaculate* is made up of two parts: the first a biography on St. Francis of Assisi and the second part on the Marian character of the Franciscan Order based on its long Marian tradition, from St. Francis to St. Maximilian Kolbe.

Not Made by Hands *by Thomas Sennott* An excellent resource book covering the two most controversial images in existence: the Holy Image of Our Lady of Guadalupe on the tilma of Juan Diego and the Sacred Image of the Crucified on the Shroud of Turin, giving scientific evidence for their authenticity and exposing the fraudulent carbon 14 test.

For the Life of the World *by Jerzy Domanski, O.F.M. Conv.* The former international director of the Knights of the Immaculata and Guardian of the City of the Immaculate in Poland examines Fr. Kolbe's Eucharistic, spiritual life as a priest and adorer of the Eucharist, all in the context of his love of the Immaculate.

Padre Pio of Pietrelcina *by Fr. Stefano Manelli, F.I.* This 144 page popular life of Padre Pio is packed with details about his life, spirituality, and charisms, by one who knew the Padre intimately. The author turned to Padre Pio for guidance in establishing a new Community, the Franciscans of the Immaculate.

Come Follow Me *by Fr. Stefano Manelli, F.I.* A book directed to any young person contemplating a Religious vocation. Informative, with many inspiring illustrations and words from the lives and writings of the Saints on the challenging vocation of total dedication in the following of Christ and His Immaculate Mother through the three vows of religion.

Mary at the Foot of the Cross I *Acts of the International Symposium on Mary, Coredemeer, Mediatrix and Advocate.* This over 400 page book on a week-long symposium held in 2000 at Ratcliffe College in England, has a whole array of outstanding Mariologists from many parts of the world. To name a few: Bishop Paul Hnilica, Fr. Bertrand De Margerie, S.J., Dr. Mark Miravalle, Fr. Stefano Manelli, F.I., Fr. Aidan Nichols, O.P. , Msgr. Arthur Calkins, and Fr. Peter Fehlner, F.I. who was the moderator. Ask about books on similar symposiums in 2001-2005.

Do You Know Our Lady *by Rev. Mother Francesca Perillo, F.I.* This handy treatise (125 pages) covers the many rich references to Mary, as prefigured in the Old Testament women and prophecies and as found in the New Testament from the Annunciation to Pentecost. Mary's role is seen ever beside her Divine Son, and the author shows how scripture supports Mary's role as Mediatrix of all Graces. Though it can be read with profit by scripture scholars, it is an easy read for everyone. Every Marian devotee should have a copy for quick reference.

SAINTS AND MARIAN SHRINE SERIES

Edited by Bro. Francis Mary, F.I.

A Handbook on Guadalupe This well researched book on Guadalupe contains 40 topical chapters by leading experts on Guadalupe with new insights and the latest scientific findings. A number of chapters deal with Our Lady's role as the patroness of the pro-life movement. Well illustrated.

St. Thérèse: Doctor of the Little Way A compendium of 32 chapters covering many unique facets about the latest Doctor of the Church by 23 authors including Fr. John Hardon, S.J., Msgr. Vernon Johnson, Sister Marie of the Trinity, OCD, Stephanè Piat. This different approach to St. Thérèse is well illustrated.

Marian Shrines of France The four major Marian shrines and apparitions of France during the 19th century: Our Lady at Rue du Bac, Paris (Miraculous Medal), La Salette, Lourdes and Pontmain shows how in the 19th century — Our Lady was checkmating our secular, Godless 20th century, introducing the present Age of Mary. Well illustrated with many color pictures.

Padre Pio - The Wonder Worker The latest on this popular saint of our times including the two inspirational homilies given by Pope John Paul II during the beatification celebration in Rome. The first part of the book is a short biography. The second is on his spirituality, charisms, apostolate of the confessional, and his great works of charity.

Marian Shrines of Italy Another in the series of "Marian Saints and Shrines," with 36 pages of colorful illustrations on over thirty of the 1500 Marian shrines in Italy. The book covers that topic with an underlying theme of the intimate and vital relationship between Mary and the Church. This is especially apparent in Catholic Italy, where the center of the Catholic Faith is found.

Special rates are available with 10% to 50% discount depending on the number of books, plus postage. For ordering books and further information on rates to book stores, schools and parishes: Academy of the Immaculate, 164 Charleston Ridge Dr., Mocksville, NC 27028, Phone/FAX (336) 751-2990, E-mail Mimike@pipeline.com. Quotations on bulk rates shipped directly by the box from the printery, contact: Franciscans of the Immaculate, P.O. Box 3003, New Bedford, MA 02741, (508) 996-8274, FAX (508) 996-8296, E-mail: ffi@marymediatrix. com., Web site, www.marymediatrix.com.